THIS
PUP
STEPS
UP!

THIS PUP STEPS UP!

A Dog Book for Kids

ANNA E. JORDAN

ROCKRIDGE
PRESS

Interior and Cover Designer: Scott Petrower
Art Producer: Tom Hood
Editor: Elizabeth Baird
Production Editor: Rachel Taenzler

Photography © Capuski/iStock, cover, p. iii; fotojagodka/iStock, back cover, p. iv; Sonsedska/iStock, p. i; Paffy69/iStock, p. iv; Dorottya_Mathe, p. 2; THEPALMER/iStock, p. 3; fizkes/iStock, p. 3; LSOphoto/iStock, p. 3; Wavebreakmedia/iStock, p. 3; cynoclub/iStock, pp 4, 5; William Mullins/Alamy, p. 6; Alistair Heap/Alamy, p. 6; Pluto/Alamy, p. 7; vauvau/iStock, pp 9, 43; PixelsEffect/iStock, p. 10; monkeybusinessimages/iStock, p. 11; editman/iStock, p. 12; Shutterstock, p 13, 18, 21, 24, 27, 29, 35, 38, 39, 41; Farlap/Alamy, pp 14, 15; Octavian Burcu/iStock, pp 16, 17; adogslifephoto/iStock, pp 19, 31; rfranca/Alamy, p. 20; Debrock44/iStock, p. 22; drbimages/iStock, p. 23; ChristinLola/iStock, pp 25, 35, damedeeso/IStock, p. 26; Anna-av/iStock, p. 28; Yuri_Arcurs/iStock, p. 30; RichLegg/iStock, p. 31; alvarez/iStock, pp 31, 43; smrm1977/iStock, p. 32; TerryJ/iStock, p. 33; FatCamera/iStock, pp 34, 36; dageldog/iStock, p. 35; ProArtWork/iStock, p. 36; kali9/iStock, p. 36; ulkas/iStock, p. 36; Peopleimages/iStock, p. 37; shironosov/iStock, p. 40; bruev/iStock, p. 40; FluxFactory/iStock, p. 40; K_Thalhofer/iStock, p. 40; fotojagodka/iStock, p. 42; yellowsarah/iStock, p. 42; Seregraff/iStock, p. 42; Thitisate Thitirojanawat/iStock, p. 42; GlobalP/iStock, pp 42, 43; mpikula/iStock, p. 42; GeraldMercier/iStock, p. 43; iStock, p. 43; sdominick/iStock, p. 44. Author Photo courtesy Sheryl Palese.

ISBN: Print 978-1-64739-848-4 | eBook 978-1-64739-849-1
R0

TO LUCY

Softest ears.
Prettiest eyes.
Smartest pup.
She is missed.

Would you like a **furry friend**

to be loyal till the end?

Then, a pup
is right for you!

Come! Let's see
what they can do.

Big
or
small,

all dogs are cuties.

Some help with important duties.

GUIDE DOG PUPPY

When a person cannot see,

a well-trained
guide dog
leads with glee.

If a person
cannot hear,

this pup
will gladly
lend
an ear.

If you're feeling sick or **BLUE**,

**this
pup**

steps up
to comfort
you!

Bark! Bark! Bark!

This dog will say,

"Here comes a truck!

Don't block the way!"

When a sheep decides to roam,

Harnessed to a sled in snow,

these pups can really go, go, go!

But not all pups
have jobs to do.

They'll clean your spills up off the floor.

They'll find the ball you throw too far.

They'll ask
for walks
with
hopeful
eyes

and help you get some exercise!

Dogs can make
new
friends
with ease.

They love to play with pals

like these!

But even good pups
like to chew . . .

They'll scatter fluff

or eat your shoe!

They'll help you get all nice and **muddy** . . .

and be your favorite
cuddle buddy!

A happy pup

will never fail

to have a joyful, **wagging** tail.

Winter,

spring,

summer,

fall,

POODLE

POMERANIAN

DACHSHUND

FRENCH BULLDOG

DALMATIAN

CHIHUAHUA

GOLDEN RETRIEVER

MIXED BREED

GERMAN SHEPHERD

HUSKY

CORGI

ABOUT THE AUTHOR

ANNA E. JORDAN was the recipient of the 2013 PEN New England Susan P. Bloom Children's Book Discovery Award and has an MFA from the Writing for Children and Young Adults program at Vermont College of Fine Arts. Her poems appear in *Babybug*, *Ladybug*, and *Highlights High Five* as well as the anthology *The Proper Way to Meet a Hedgehog and Other How-To Poems* (Candlewick Press, 2019).

CPSIA information can be obtained
at www.ICGtesting.com
Printed in the USA
LVHW021135171220
674420LV00001B/3